Love Your Finches

Love Your Finches

Chris Blackwell

W. Foulsham & Co. Ltd.
London • New York • Toronto • Cape Town • Sydney

W. Foulsham & Company Limited
Yeovil Road, Slough, Berkshire, SL1 4JH

ISBN 0-572-01387-6

Printed in Spain by Cayfosa, Barcelona.
Dep. Leg. B-27227-1986

The author would like to acknowledge the help and
assistance of Mr. Bob Gibbon while compiling the
notes and photographs relating to Bengalese.

Page 2:   Chestnut and White Bengalese

Contents

1 **Introduction**

Zebra Finches and Bengalese Finches are both small foreign seed-eating birds which, through their willingness to breed in cages and aviaries, are now regarded as domesticated species. Both are social by nature and should not be kept as solitary birds. They are quite hardy birds and do not require 'hot house' temperatures in order to survive. They are ideal for the beginner as they only require a simple diet and their general management is easy.

In the main, Zebra Finches originate from Australia where they are widespread in most areas where food and water can be found. They live in flocks or colonies and their breeding activities are triggered by rainfall rather than by seasonal changes. This means that they will usually breed at anytime of year.

Due to the large numbers of birds bred in captivity and a ban on exporting wild birds from Australia, virtually all the birds available now come from domesticated stocks. When birds are bred in controlled conditions it is usual for mutations to be produced. Zebra Finches are no exception. The variety of colours available make it quite possible to maintain an interesting and varied collection although only one species is kept.

The majority of cock Zebra Finches show cheek patches, side flankings and breast barring, which are absent in hens, and this means they can be easily sexed from their visual appearance alone.

The origins of Bengalese are somewhat uncertain as they have no exact counterpart in the wild, and the breed was developed many years ago. It is thought that they were produced by hybridising between two or more similar species of birds related to the Mannikin family.

There are various different colours of Bengalese readily available, ranging from deep chocolate to pure white, and they too can form an interesting collection without the addition of other species. Bengalese are not as easily sexed as are Zebra Finches, there being no visual difference between cocks and hens. Sexing is only possible by observation of their courtship display and therefore it may be difficult to acquire a true breeding pair initially.

For anyone who wishes to become involved in the competitive exhibition of birds, both Zebra Finches and Bengalese are excellent subjects. Quite large numbers of both species can be seen at many cage bird shows. Naturally not everyone is interested in showing their birds, but these events provide the means to meet more experienced owners who are usually only too pleased to offer advice on any problems which may arise. Zebra Finches and Bengalese Finches will be found to be charming birds full of personality and character. Many satisfying and relaxing hours can be spent simply observing their antics.

2 **Choosing Your Finches**

Both Zebra Finches and Bengalese can be bought from most good pet shops. They are available at most times of year, but supplies tend to be more plentiful during mid-summer. It is always advisable to inspect the birds before making any purchase. Birds which do not seem to be fully fit must be avoided, as Zebra Finches and Bengalese should be lively and full of life and vigour. Birds that remain inactive for long periods, continually rough their feathers up, as though cold, and shun the company of other birds, are probably unwell and may only live for a few days.

Colour depends largely on the individual preference of the buyer as all colours require the same general management and feeding. However should one specific colour be required then it may be necessary to contact a specialist breeder.

Normally when buying birds breeding pairs will be required and therefore you need to be able to differentiate between cocks and hens. In the case of Zebra Finches (with the exception of Whites) cock birds are marked differently to hens and therefore the selection of true pairs should pose few problems. Initially it is usual to buy pairs of the same colour, as the intermating of two different colours can result in only Normal or Grey youngsters being produced.

Bengalese cannot be sexed by their appearance, or variations in size. Cock birds can be identified by their display ritual. This involves the bird adopting a more dominant attitude than usual, uttering a distinctive, squeaky, song and the tail being carried in a more raised position than normal. However, cock birds will display to each other and just because a bird does not display, it does not mean it is necessarily a hen. Nevertheless, once this problem has been overcome, owners should be able to sex their own birds more reliably by careful observation over a longer period of time, and a collection of breeding pairs can soon be established.

Often birds for sale will be wearing a closed metal ring on one leg. The colour of this ring can help to determine the age of an individual bird. As they are closed rings they can only be fitted to young birds in the nest and if they are issued by a specialist society a different colour of ring will be used each year. In Britain the following cycle of ring colours is used: Violet, Yellow, Turquoise, Red, Gold, Pink, Dark Blue, Orange and Green, commencing with Violet in 1985. The cycle is repeated every nine years. These rings also allow for precise identification of the birds and the person who bred them. If possible young birds should be purchased as most Zebra Finches and Bengalese only have a limited life span of about three or four years.

Having obtained your Finches, no matter from which source, they should be housed separately from other birds for at least two weeks, to ensure they are not diseased in any way. Additionally newly acquired birds should be treated with a mite powder, made specifically for birds. A further course of treatment must then be administered seven days after the first application.

If it is possible to obtain advice from a more experienced breeder this can be most useful and contacts can often be made through local bird societies.

Close ringing small finches

The ring is placed over the 3 forward pointing toes and positioned over the ball of the foot

The ring is carefully drawn over the back claw until positioned against the knee joint

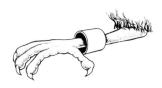

The back claw is eased free from the ring allowing it to be fitted correctly to the leg

A Black-eyed White Bengalese

A pair of Self Chocolate Bengalese

3 Housing

Before buying any birds it is essential to ensure that they can be properly housed when brought home. Having decided to keep Bengalese or Zebra Finches, provision must be made to accommodate at least a pair of these birds. Should breeding be successfully achieved, youngsters will also require suitable housing. Even so, it is quite possible to start by keeping a pair of birds in the home, and if your interest continues to develop, an outdoor aviary can be considered later.

Zebra Finches and Bengalese are best housed in a box-type cage which must be at least 60 cm in length, 38 cm in height and 38 cm (2ft × 15in × 15in) from back to front. The top, back, bottom and sides of these cages are solid, with only the front being of wire. The most suitable is a budgerigar front. These have no head-holes and have a large hinged door, which allows nest boxes for breeding purposes to be placed inside easily. Cages should also have a removable sliding tray at the bottom as this allows much easier cleaning of the cage. All cages must contain two perches of 6–12mm (¼–½in) in diameter and these are usually positioned at each end of the cage, allowing a clearance of 7–10 cm between the perch and the cage wall.

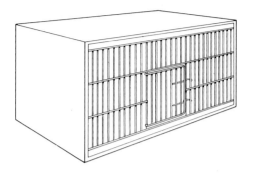

Cage suitable for a pair of Zebra Finches or Bengalese

Cages can be bought ready made from many pet shops. It is also possible to buy the wire cage fronts separately and then construct a cage to your own specifications. With a little thought it may be possible to make the cage an attractive feature in the home by incorporating it into a wall unit or bookcase. Armed with a few basic carpentry skills and the necessary tools, cage construction poses few problems.

The positioning of the cage within the home must be given careful thought. Kitchens are not usually suitable places to house birds and cages must never be placed close to or directly above heaters. The best position is one which receives plenty of natural light and allows the owner to view the birds easily.

For the person wishing to house birds in a garden aviary, these too can be bought ready made or constructed from basic raw materials. The design must include shelter for the birds during bad weather and a frost-free area during the winter months. In many cases this will mean providing supplementary heating within a shelter attached to the aviary. Electric heating is the safest and most convenient and can be controlled by means of a thermostat.

Supplementary lighting can also be provided, and this can make feeding simpler, especially during the winter months. To prevent the birds being startled when the lights are switched off suddenly, dimmers – which reduce the level of light gradually – can also be fitted.

Aviaries must be sited on firm level ground free from standing water, and all timber used for outdoor constructions must be treated with

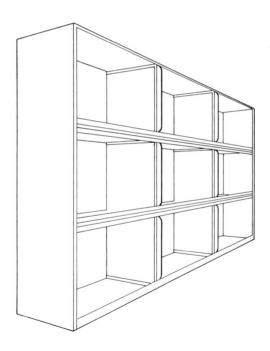

A block of 9 cages which can be converted into 3 large flight cages by removing the dividing panels

preservative. The floor should be gravel or concrete as these are easier to maintain. One side of the aviary, usually the north facing wall, should be solid to offer the birds some protection. In order to protect feeding areas at least part of the aviary roof will need to be covered. Corrugated plastic sheeting is ideal for this, especially on aviaries which have a sloping roof.

Another wise precaution is to fit a safety porch around the outside door of the aviary which will prevent birds accidentally escaping while you are entering or leaving the flight. It is not usually practical to construct an aviary which is less than 1·8 m. in height as easy access is required on the part of the birdkeeper to carry out various aspects of general management and maintenance. Perching and cover can be provided by using cut twigs and foliage, which can be positioned to your own requirements and replaced when necessary.

However, a garden aviary can have its restrictions during the breeding season as such a structure will only accommodate about six breeding pairs. A much more effective use of space can be realised by combining an outdoor birdroom and aviary, breeding pairs being housed in cages and the aviary used for youngsters and surplus stock.

A good quality garden shed fitted with windows can be converted into an excellent birdroom. In order to eliminate unwanted draughts most birdrooms are lined throughout with either hardboard or plywood. Some form of insulating material can be incorporated between the lining and the walls and roof, which will help to minimise heating costs. However birdrooms must never be stuffy and some

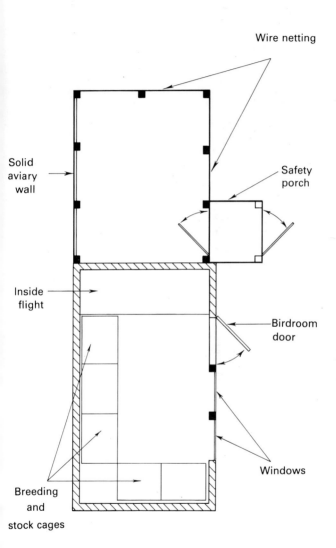

Wire netting

Solid aviary wall

Safety porch

Inside flight

Birdroom door

Windows

Breeding and stock cages

17

form of ventilation should be included. In warm weather additional ventilation can be provided by making a wire door for the birdroom to replace the normal solid wooden door. Windows must be protected by wire netting in case of accidental breakages, not only to prevent birds escaping if a cage door has been left open, but also to prevent entry by unwanted visitors such as cats. A birdroom for Zebra Finches and Bengalese should be kept at a minimum temperature of about 5°C/40°F and in order to achieve this some form of heating may be needed. Lighting is also useful for the darker days of winter. Forms of heating and lighting, other than electric, tend to be unreliable and can give off fumes which are harmful to birds, so choose an electric heater.

The interior layout of birdrooms can vary depending on the requirements of each birdkeeper. Usually, six breeding cages will be needed and these must measure at least 60 cm long, 38 cm high and 38 cm deep (2ft × 15in × 15in) each. When a birdroom is to be used in conjunction with an outdoor aviary, some form of access between the two will need to be provided. If possible the outdoor aviary should be divided into two parts so that cocks and hens can be housed separately when not breeding. Often beginners will underestimate the number of breeding cages which will be required. Although adequate provisions are made for birds initially, many people are reluctant to part with the young they breed during the first two or three years. This means increasing the numbers of breeding pairs kept each year and it is not unusual to end up with a stock of about twenty breeding pairs.

A nest of young Bengalese containing Self Chocolate and Chocolate and White chicks at fourteen days of age.

A baby Self Fawn Bengalese chick at fourteen days of age.

4 **Feeding**

The basic diet required by both Zebra Finches and Bengalese Finches is very similar and easy to provide. The essential elements are seed, water and grit, and although various other foods will also be appreciated, it is important to ensure the basic diet is of good quality.

Seed

A suitable seed mixture, consisting of various different millets and small canary seed, can be bought from most good pet shops. Alternatively each type of seed can be bought separately and a mixture made up to the exact proportions required. Zebra Finches tend to select a larger proportion of the smaller seeds, while Bengalese often prefer the larger millet. A good basic mixture to try initially would be five parts panicum millet, three parts pearl white millet, two parts canary seed, half a part japanese millet and half a part dakota millet. Any seeds which remain uneaten should be reduced in quantity, while those which are always eaten can be increased. Normally seed for small finches is supplied in open pots placed inside cages and aviaries, rather than in seed hoppers which tend to be designed for larger types of birds. It will be necessary to top

A pair of Chestnut Flanked White Zebra Finches

An exhibition type Fawn Hen Zebra Finch

up seed pots daily, but before adding fresh seed, remove any discarded seed husks. The simplest method of doing this is to blow the surface of the seed gently, taking care that husks do not fly into your eyes. Being small birds both Zebra Finches and Bengalese eat very often throughout the day and they should never be kept in conditions where they do not always have access to a suitable seed supply.

Water

Fresh water must also be available at all times and this can either be provided in open water dishes or in plastic drinkers, which clip to the outside of the cage. Open water dishes may be a problem as the birds love to bathe and within a few hours very little water will remain for drinking. Plastic drinkers prevent bathing, but even so it is advisable to provide fresh water every day. In addition open water dishes which will allow the birds to bathe should be provided two or three times each week.

Water is often used to supply birds with various tonics and medicines. This being the case, baths will need to be removed and water supplied in plastic drinkers, for the entire course of treatment. It is pointless providing a water-based tonic if the birds can use it as bath water. Also if birds have a choice of treated and untreated water, the vast majority will simply drink the untreated water.

Grit

A regular supply of grit is an essential dietary ingredient for finches. They need it to grind the seed into digestible particles inside the crop. Without grit the digestive system will be seriously impaired, resulting in a loss of general fitness and condition. Most forms of grit also contain vital trace elements and minerals which are required in regular small amounts for good health. Additionally hens require a plentiful supply of calcium to produce properly shelled eggs. This is particularly important prior to and during the breeding season. Birds should also be supplied with mineralised grit at all times, and this can be complemented by adding a little limestone grit. The grit pot must be topped up regularly every week, even though adequate supplies may seem to be available as the birds will search for particles of the preferred composition and size and leave the rest.

A further source of calcium is cuttlefish bone, which is enjoyed by both Bengalese and Zebra Finches. This should be available in its solid form at all times and can be given in powdered form in the grit pot for six to eight weeks before the breeding season, to ensure that hens have an adequate supply of calcium.

Another element which can be provided in small quantities for all birds is charcoal. This helps to 'sweeten' the digestive system although it should not be given to excess.

Rearing Food

A suitable rearing food should be provided for breeding birds as this will help them produce healthy chicks. Various brands of rearing food, which only require the addition of warm water, can be purchased. These should be mixed to a crumbly consistency. Any uneaten food must be removed within 24 hours. Wheatgerm bread mixed with a little milk is also an excellent rearing food, but care must be taken to ensure it does not become sour, especially during warm weather.

Whatever form of rearing food is selected, birds should be given the chance to sample it before being faced with the task of rearing youngsters. Ideally it should be given at least once a fortnight throughout the year, with the supply increased as required before and during the breeding season. Many owners will devise their own rearing food, adding little extras which they feel to be of benefit, but initially it is best to start with a simple food.

Greenfood

Greenfood will be appreciated by most finches and this can be provided in the form of lettuce, cabbage, Brussels sprouts, mustard cress or dandelion leaves. Small amounts of sweet apple, grated carrot or orange can also be offered, and these will help to promote general health. During the summer months wild seeds (seeding grasses or ratstail plantain seed spikes) can often be gathered, and these will be a welcome addition to the basic diet. However, when collecting food found growing wild, make sure it has not been treated with any harmful chemicals, or fouled by dogs or cats. Equally, wild food must never be collected from the sides of busy roads as it is bound to be affected by exhaust fumes. Should there be any doubt about the source of wild food, then it is much better to leave it alone.

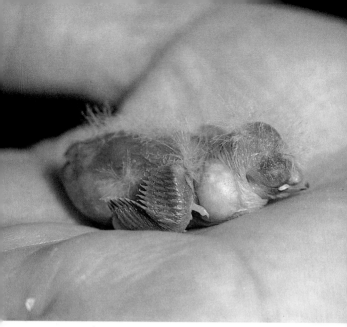

A baby Fawn Zebra Finch – five days old

A baby Normal Pied Zebra Finch – eight days old

During the breeding season greenfood can give rise to problems as some birds may use it to cover eggs or small youngsters, with fatal consequences. No form of perishable food should be left in cages or aviaries for more than 24 hours as it can be a health hazard once it starts to decay.

Tonics

Most breeders will provide their birds with extra tonics before the breeding season. It is essential that birds are not deficient in vitamin D at this time as it promotes healthy growth in young birds. It can be provided by using soluble vitamin products which are added to the drinking water. Another source of vitamin D often used is cod liver oil and this is provided by mixing it with the basic seed mixture. Ask your local pet shop for details. Once birds have settled to their breeding duties the supply of tonics is best discontinued, in case the birds become too fit and refuse to carry out the tasks of sitting eggs and rearing youngsters properly.

Millet sprays

Many pet shops sell millet sprays, which are seeding heads of millet, and while they contain the same seed provided in the basic diet, birds will often enjoy feeding from a millet spray, rather than a seed pot.

5 General Management

In addition to providing birds with food and water there are several other aspects of general management to be undertaken. Birds will always prefer to be kept in well maintained, hygienic conditions, which help to promote general fitness and limit the possibility of disease or infection.

Cages require cleaning regularly, ideally once a week. This is made much easier if they are fitted with removable sliding trays. Once clean the trays need to be recovered with sand, sawdust or paper, as preferred. For birds kept in the home, paper is usually the most convenient form of floor covering, as sand and sawdust easily become scattered outside the cage.

In a birdroom sand or sawdust will probably be a better cage floor covering as natural sand contains elements which will be of benefit to the birds, while sawdust tends to be cleaner and absorbs moisture more effectively. Care must be taken to ensure that any sand or sawdust used for cage floors is free from contamination by oil, wood preservatives or other harmful chemicals. When birds are breeding it may be best to clean cages a little less frequently and unnecessary disturbance should be avoided while birds are incubating eggs or have very small youngsters.

All perches must be kept clean and well maintained. Any loose perches should be replaced or modified so that they are securely fixed in placed. Perches should never be positioned directly over food containers as this will allow the birds to foul the food with their droppings. Dirty perches may be scraped clean or washed and scrubbed in warm soapy water and then rinsed thoroughly. All perches should be soaked for about twelve hours in a mild disinfectant solution, rinsed thoroughly and allowed to dry, at least twice each year.

It is preferable to provide perches of varying thicknesses for birds as this permits them to exercise their feet fully. Ideally perches varying in thickness from about 6–12mm ($\frac{1}{4}$ –$\frac{1}{2}$ in) in diameter are suitable for Zebra Finches and Bengalese. Natural twigs tend to offer more variation in thickness but can often become loose as they dry out. Dowelling perches can be sand-papered to provide more variety in thickness.

Seed dishes, drinkers, baths, grit hoppers and other utensils will require washing thoroughly at least once a month. Containers used for supplying rearing food must be washed out every time they are used.

Cages and aviaries must be washed down thoroughly at least twice a year and will require painting annually unless made from laminated boards. Emulsion paint is probably the most convenient type of paint to use, and whatever type of paint is used, it is important to ensure that it contains no toxic elements.

Used nest boxes must be scraped out thoroughly, well washed in warm soapy water and sprayed with a mild disinfectant solution,

A baby Fawn Pied Zebra Finch – twelve days old

A baby Chestnut Flanked White Zebra Finch – twelve days old

before being stored for the following season. Birdrooms should be kept neat and tidy at all times, utensils not being used need to be stored out of the way and foodstuffs kept in ventilated containers. Sloppiness will encourage the attention of vermin which need to be discouraged at all costs.

Every day you should observe each individual bird for a few moments. Any birds which appear 'off colour' will need to be removed from the company of other birds. Their condition may have been caused by fighting with other birds in the same cage, in which case they will soon make a full recovery when placed on their own. Occasionally birds will catch some form of disease and there is a much better chance of a successful cure if the symptoms are noticed at an early stage.

Any birds with dirty feet or heavily soiled feathers should be caught and gently washed in warm water until clean. The use of soap or shampoo to wash birds is not recommended for inexperienced owners as the natural oils may be removed from the plumage and make birds particularly susceptible to the cold.

To the beginner it may seem quite complicated remembering to carry out all the necessary tasks. However, by employing a set routine it will soon be found to be relatively easy to care for your birds.

A variety of toys 'designed' for cage birds can be purchased, however these are of little use to anyone keeping Zebra Finches or Bengalese, as they will be totally ignored by the vast majority of these birds. The practise of allowing birds out of their cage for exercise is also not commonly employed with these birds. They can rarely be trained to become finger tame, unless very young birds are acquired and a great deal of time is spent gaining their confidence, and they will seldom return to their cage without being physically caught. It is much better to provide a cage which is large enough to give the birds all the exercise they need and allow them to remain within the sanctuary of their own 'territory', where they feel safe and secure.

6 Health

With proper care and attention Zebra Finches and Bengalese will enjoy a fit and healthy life whether kept in a cage or aviary. However there are a number of complaints which will be encountered from time to time and most of these are easily treated.

Egg binding is obviously a condition only suffered by hens and occurs when the bird has difficulty in passing an egg. It is often associated with damp, cold conditions and is caused by birds having insufficient calcium or vitaming D, or both, in their diet. Affected birds will sit fluffed up, often on the cage floor, appear to be in a distressed condition and are usually 'thick' around the vent. The cure is to place birds in a 'hospital' cage at about 24°C/75°F, together with seed, water and grit. After a few hours of being in warmer surroundings the bird will show signs of recovery and once the offending egg has been laid, most will appear to return to full fitness. It is important to allow the bird a 'hardening off' period before it is returned to its usual cage, and this is done by gradually reducing the temperature of the hospital cage over two or three days. If you do not possess a purpose built hospital cage then birds can be brought indoors and kept in a warm place, but not where the bird might be affected by harmful fumes from a heater.

Under no circumstances should one attempt to dislodge the egg physically. Although the cure given is quite effective, prevention by the feeding of the correct diet is much to be preferred. Birds which are breeding when they become egg bound will need to be parted from their mate for at least four weeks and this, of course, will adversely affect the chances of producing youngsters.

When birds are kept in cold, damp and draughty quarters they will be susceptible to chills. Symptoms shown in affected birds are very similar to those displayed by birds which are egg bound. The treatment is also very similar, except that it will usually take the affected bird longer to recover and it will also require a longer 'hardening off' period.

'Going light' is a term used to describe birds which display the general symptoms of colds and chills, but these are also accompanied by a rapid and severe loss of weight. The cause is not yet fully understood and many affected birds will recover if placed in a 'hospital' cage at 24°C/75°F. Unfortunately most will fail to maintain this recovery when returned to their normal cage and additional treatment will be required. You should consult a vet for proper guidance.

Feather mite often affects birds which are kept in outdoor aviaries. These mites can be detected by examining the large tail and wing feathers against a light source. If they are holed or eaten away, especially around the central spine, then the bird is infested with mite and must be treated. Various preparations specially designed for cage birds, such as an anti mite aerosol spray and a mite powder, are available from most good pet shops.

Scaly face appears as a white or yellowish crust on the beaks of some birds. This too is caused by mite. A proprietry brand of scaly face cream can be purchased at most pet shops and if used to the manufacturers recommendations will completely cure the problem.

Swollen or sore feet may give cause for concern from time to time and these can usually be effectively treated using scaly face cream or clear iodine solution. Daily treatment will be required, bathing the feet gently, and after about one week the condition should be greatly improved, if not cured altogether. When birds have overgrown claws or nails it will be necessary to trim them. This is a relatively simple task and can be done using a sharp pair of nail scissors. If the nail is viewed against the light a red vein inside the nail will be clearly visible. This vein must not be cut. If in doubt consult the vet.

Eye infections may be caused by fighting, or may be due to draughts, and the condition can be aggravated if the birds rub the affected eye. Careful bathing in a solution of boracic powder on a daily basis will help to ease the irritation and the problem will usually be cured after about seven days treatment. If the condition persists then professional advice from a veterinary surgeon may be required.

On average Bengalese and Zebra Finches have a life expectancy of three to four years. Naturally some will not attain their full life expectancy, while others have been known to successfully rear youngsters at ten years of age!

A nest of young Zebra Finches

Normal Pied

7 **Breeding**

Zebra Finches and Bengalese show a great willingness to breed, given very little encouragement. Even when kept in the home pairs will attempt to go to nest and many will successfully rear youngsters. Because conditions indoors are less harsh than those in an outdoor aviary it is possible they will breed out of season. Should the hen of a pair be laying eggs regularly then the birds must be given opportunity to go through the full breeding cycle. Failure to permit this can lead to the hen laying eggs continually, which is bound to affect her general health and fitness.

For those keeping small finches in outdoor accommodation the best time to start breeding activities is early spring. A minimum temperature of 5°C/40°F should be maintained when birds are breeding and often better results are obtained if the temperature can be kept above 10°C/50°F.

Various different types of nesting site can be provided for small finches, but the most commonly used are wooden nest boxes fitted with a removable top to allow inspection of eggs and chicks. These nest boxes can be easily constructed using plywood. They should be about 15 cm × 15 cm × 15 cm (6 in × 6 in × 6 in ×) with the top 5 cm of the front being left open across the full width to allow access for

Normal

Fawn and White

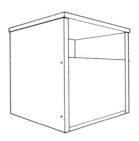

A typical nest box for Zebra Finches or Bengalese

the birds. Before being placed in the cage or aviary nest boxes need to be well filled with dry grass and moss so that it is level with the opening in the front of the box. Where a single pair is housed in a cage, one nest box is quite sufficient, but in an aviary where several breeding pairs are being housed, at least two nest boxes for each pair must be provided. Nest boxes should not be directly above or below each other and no closer than 30 cm. apart.

Having paired birds together, and providing they settle well, the first egg should be laid seven days after mating. If eggs are laid sooner there is a chance they will be infertile. Incubation usually commences on the day the third egg is laid, and this duty, as well as feeding, is shared by both the cock and hen. A full clutch can range from four to eight eggs and they will usually 'turn' after five full days of incubation. This means that if the egg is fertile the embryo will have started to develop visibly. If the egg is fertile red veins can be seen inside the egg. Infertile eggs appear clear or may have a slight yellowish tinge. If no evidence of 'turning' can be seen after seven full days of incubation, the clutch can be discarded and the birds allowed to produce another round of eggs. When handling eggs, make sure your hands are warm and do not hold them too close to the light source as this could damage the embryo.

Providing all goes well, Zebra Finch eggs usually hatch after twelve to fourteen days incubation, while Bengalese eggs take about two days longer to hatch. Should Zebra Finch eggs fail to hatch after being incubated for sixteen days, and Bengalese eggs after eighteen days, they are unlikely to do so and can be discarded. This can be due to various causes, but the most common is that the parent birds have let the eggs become chilled at some stage in their development and the chicks inside have perished. If birds are disturbed at night eggs can become chilled and for this reason many birdkeepers keep a low wattage electric light burning all night so that parent birds can find their way back to the nest if they are disturbed.

Although a pair of birds may have laid eight eggs, it is unreasonable to expect them to rear this number of youngsters. Once five of the eggs have hatched, surplus eggs can be removed, certainly six youngsters in a single nest is quite sufficient.

Rearing food should be provided for breeding pairs on the evening before their eggs are due to hatch, and then once or twice daily while they have young to feed. With proper feeding the chicks will grow and develop quite quickly and by the time they are about seven days old it is usually possible for the owner to determine what colours have been produced. At fourteen days old the young will be feathering nicely and most leave the nest at about 21 days of age. Just before fledging great care must be taken when inspecting nest boxes as one false move can cause the young to bolt and it can be very tricky returning them to the nest box.

Youngsters which have been well fed by their parents will usually be able to feed themselves at 28 days old. Some young take a little longer to master the art of shelling seed. This can be a critical time especially if parent birds are keen to go to nest again and some may stop feeding their young just a day or two before they are able to feed properly. Often the only possible course of action is to remove the hen bird from the breeding cage and hope that the cock will then recommence his parental duties. Most birds will oblige and feed the young until they are self sufficient. This being achieved the young can be separated and the hen returned to her mate.

When young have been removed from the care of their parents they should be allowed at least two weeks in a stock cage before being placed in an outdoor aviary. The opportunity should also be taken to remove the old nest box and replace it with a clean one well filled with fresh nesting material. In the case of Zebra Finches any eggs which have been laid can be safely discarded as the parent birds will soon produce another round of eggs. Bengalese are slightly less prolific with regard to egg laying and unless the eggs seem to be damaged, it is wisest to retain them. If a single pair of birds rear two good rounds of youngsters in a season they have rewarded you amply and deserve a rest. Most pairs will attempt to rear three or four rounds of young if left un-checked, but to allow such a state of affairs is simply being greedy and can affect breeding performances in future years.

8 **Varieties**

There are various different colours and mutations of Zebra Finches and Bengalese widely available. When any species of bird is kept in controlled conditions it is quite usual for mutations to be produced and often these can be isolated and so form the basis of new colour forms. In the wild such mutations will rarely survive as most are easy targets for predators and, even if they manage to breed, very often the young produced will revert back to the original colour form.

Normal

The domestic counterpart of the wild Zebra Finch is the Grey or Normal form, and it is from these that all the other colours have been derived. The basic body colour of Normals on the head, neck, back and wings is mid to dark grey. Both cocks and hens have black tails barred with white and black tear marks below the eye. Additionally cock birds display various markings which are absent on hens. They have dark orange or chestnut coloured cheek patches, and beneath the beak and down the throat and breast are thin lateral black stripes which terminate in a broader black band. This is known as the breast bar and should extend across the full width of the chest. The majority

A pair of Normal Zebra Finches

An exhibition type Normal Pied Cock Zebra Finch

of cocks have bright coral red beaks and red-orange feet and legs. In hens these features tend to be a shade paler in colour.

Very few normal Zebra Finches are genetically pure in colour and most will carry one or more colour mutations concealed in their genetic make up. Such birds do not necessarily differ visually from pure bred birds and the fact that they are carrying other colours will only come to light by their breeding results. For the beginner the production of unexpected colours can create extra interest during the breeding season.

Fawn

The Fawn mutation was one of the first to appear in captivity and has also been reported in the wild from time to time. Fawn Zebra Finches are very popular and on the show bench they are often firm favourites to take the leading honours. Fawns differ from Normals in that those areas of feathering which are usually grey, are replaced with plumage of a fawn colour. The other characteristic markings remain virtually unaltered except for being very slightly paler in shade.

Originally Fawns were known as Cinnamon Zebra Finches, but because the term cinnamon is generally applied to yellow birds, the term Fawn was felt to be more accurate. The exact shade of Fawn present in each individual bird can vary quite considerably from light brown through to pale fawn.

A pair of Fawn Zebra Finches

An exhibition type Fawn Cock Zebra Finch

Pied

The variegated mutation of Zebra Finch is usually called Pied and it is a very attractive and popular colour form especially in mixed collections. Pieds vary from other Zebra Finches in that random areas of white feathering appear in areas of plumage which usually are coloured. In some birds the pied markings may only consist of a few white flight feathers or a small white bib beneath the beak, but others can be almost totally white in appearance. The inheritance of pied marking patterns is quite random, making it possible for a pair of dark Pieds to produce relatively light Pied youngsters. Due to the popularity of Pieds, many of the Zebra Finches sold in pet shops will either be visual Pieds or carry the Pied factor hidden in their genetical make up. It is quite common to produce visual Pied youngsters from two birds which do not display pied markings.

White

When first produced many Whites suffered from grey or fawn mantling on their backs but this has largely been overcome by breeders producing White Pieds. The effect of combining the two colour forms has been to breed Whites of a much purer colour. Although a few Albino Zebra Finches have been produced, the vast majority of Whites are not Albinos as they have dark eyes. Sexing can be a problem with Whites as they display no characteristic markings, therefore they are usually sexed by their beak colour, the majority of cocks having brighter red beaks than do hens.

A pair of Normal Pied Zebra Finches

A White Cock Zebra Finch

Chestnut Flanked White

Chestnut Flanked White Zebra Finches should not be confused with White Zebra Finches, as they are two totally unrelated mutations. Ideally a Chestnut Flanked White should retain the characteristic markings displayed by Normals, but have the grey areas of feathering replaced with white plumage. It is inevitable that some dilution of markings, particularly cheek patches, occurs and the white general feathering on the back and wings will contain at least a slight tinge of grey fawn. Nevertheless, selective breeding by specialist fanciers has produced a vast improvement in this breed since it first appeared.

Lightback

A colour which is very closely related to Chestnut Flanked Whites is the Lightback Zebra Finch. Basically these birds are a form of dilute and while the mutation can be produced in both Normal and Fawn forms, Normal Lightbacks are much more plentiful than Fawn Lightbacks. The particular feature of the breed is that while the characteristic black marks remain very prominent, other colours are noticeably diluted. Ideally the general body colour of these birds should be a light silvery grey, although there is tendency for hens to be a shade darker than cock birds.

Dilutes

The most common form of dilute Zebra Finches was the Dominant variety, and the term dominant refers to their genetical breeding characteristics. Dilute Normals are known

A Dominant Silver Cock Zebra Finch

A Dominant Cream Cock Zebra Finch

as Silvers, while dilute Fawns are called Creams. These dilute forms show a uniform dilution of all the colours and markings displayed by their undiluted counterparts. The most sought after Dominant Silvers are those whose general body colour is a light silvery grey. Dominant Creams should be an even cream shade on the head, neck, back and wings, with characteristic markings being diluted correspondingly.

Penguin

The Penguin variety of Zebra Finch varies from other forms in that the tear marks and breast barring are totally absent in cock birds, and hens, in addition to showing no tear marks, have white cheek patches. Both cocks and hens have silvery grey tails barred with white and the general body colour is paler than usual with the large flight feathers showing a lacing effect. It is possible to breed Penguin varieties of all other colours, although Normal Penguins and Fawn Penguins tend to show the unusual marking pattern to best advantage.

Yellowbeak

A Yellowbeak mutation has been produced. It is probably most effective when combined with dilute mutations, and only Yellowbeak Whites tend to have a truly yellow beak.

Other varieties

A number of other Zebra Finch mutations have been produced and these include Black Breasted, Orange Breasted and Created Zebra Finches. However these colours are rarely

A Self Chocolate Bengalese

available and are often sold at excessively high prices. For the beginner they are not particularly suitable subjects and are therefore best left alone.

Many of the commonly available colours can be combined to produce birds which show the characteristics of more than one mutation, such as Yellowbeak Silver Pieds or Fawn Penguin Pieds. Birds can carry factors for a number of different mutations and youngsters of unexpected colours are often bred. The practise of breeding unusual combination colours can be very interesting and will produce a varied collection of birds.

Bengalese Self Chocolate

As there is no wild counterpart to the Bengalese it is more difficult to determine which colour is the normal form. Generally the Self Chocolate variety is regarded as the normal and, where possible, the breeding characteristics of other colours are compared to this variety. Self is a term used to describe birds which show no white feathering or variegated markings. A bird showing even just one white feather or a pied mark on the beak or legs, must be classified as a variegated bird.

Self Chocolates should be a dark even chocolate colour on the head, neck, back and wings, with the tail also being dark. Beneath and to the sides of the beak is a very dark mask. The cheeks and upper breast are chocolate decorated with lighter markings which often take the form of scalloping on the breast. The underparts from the breast to the vent are similar in shade to the light markings on the

A Self Fawn Bengalese

breast and are ticked with darker chocolate markings. The area from the vent to the base of the tail is dark and usually flecked with lighter markings. The feet and legs should also be dark, as should the upper part of the beak, the lower mandible being a metallic grey colour. Some birds tend to be a golden shade on the neck and back, but generally the darker specimens are preferred.

Self Fawn

The Self Fawn mutation is a very popular form of Bengalese. The markings on Self Fawns are as those displayed by Self Chocolates except that general body colour is reduced to fawn and the beak, legs and feet are a pale horn colour. Variations in the shade of fawn displayed do occur and usually those of a deep, rich fawn colour are preferred. Many birds carry the Fawn mutation in hidden form and it is not unusual to breed Fawn youngsters from a pair of Chocolates.

Self Chestnut

The Self Chestnut is closely related to the Self Chocolate and for many years it was thought to be a form of Dilute Chocolate. This theory has now been discounted and Chestnuts are regarded as a separate mutation. Markings are very similar to the Self Chocolate except that the general body colour is a shade lighter. The beak, legs and feet are similar to those of Self Chocolates, and are not reduced to the pale horn shade displayed by Fawns. The ideal colour for Chestnuts is a shade half way between Chocolate and Fawn. However, due to

A Self Chestnut Bengalese

variations in colour, some are as dark as pale Chocolates and others as pale as dark Fawns.

Variegated

The most commonly seen mutation of Bengalese is the Variegated or Pied form and this can be produced in all other colours. Because so many birds carry the variegated mutation in hidden form, breeders should never be surprised when birds marked with white feathers crop up in nests of youngsters produced from two Selfs. The term variegated or pied is not generally accepted. Variegated Chocolates are known as Chocolate and Whites, variegated Fawns as Fawn and Whites and variegated Chestnuts as Chestnut and Whites, etc. The pattern of markings displayed by these birds is quite random and can vary from just a few white feathers, to examples where the bird is almost totally white with only small areas of normally coloured feathering.

Dilute

It is possible to produce dilute forms of all self and variegated colours of Bengalese. Dilute Chocolates are often referred to as Silvers, while other forms are simply known as Dilute Chestnuts and Dilute Fawns. The degree of dilution shown varies considerably and the paler birds tend to be preferred.

Many dilutes are variegated, although the white markings are not particularly noticeable, due to the general paler body colour of the dilutes. The beak colour of diluted birds is often the only safe method of differentiating between Dilute Fawns and Dilute Chestnuts,

Silver and White or Dilute Chocolate and
White Bengalese

A pair of Dilute Fawn and White Bengalese

Fawns having pale beaks, while Chestnuts have dark beaks. Usually Dilute Chocolates or Silvers are a little darker than Dilute Chestnuts but there will always be those individuals which cannot be accurately identified unless their exact parentage is known.

Whites

Albino

Should Albinos be produced from two normally marked birds they are bound to be hens. As with other Albino forms of livestock, these birds are quite probably more delicate physically than birds showing normal pigmentation. They are, however, attractive additions to a mixed collection, especially one containing a predominance of dark birds, where the pure white birds will help to highlight the various marking patterns shown by the other colours.

Crested

The final mutation of Bengalese which is generally available is the Crested form. These birds can occur in any colour and are different from non-crested birds in that they have a small corona shaped crest on the head.

When exhibiting Crested Bengalese it is important to note that the definition of a pair consists of one Crested bird and one Non-Crested bird of the same colour.

A Crested Chocolate and White Bengalese

_9_ Showing

Although Zebra Finches and Bengalese are ideal birds for the beginner, both can be bred to the highest of exhibition standards if desired. The art of showing birds in competition can prove to be a most interesting extension to the hobby. Not only is there the promise of winning prize cards and rosettes if your birds are good enough, attending shows also enables you to meet new friends who share a common interest in finches.

The rules and standards governing the exhibition of Zebra Finches and Bengalese in Britain are laid down by the Zebra Finch Society and the National Bengalese Fanciers Association, respectively. The aim of both clubs is to promote the keeping, breeding and exhibition of their own particular species and their membership is open to anyone interested in these species of birds. In addition to the national clubs there are also a number of area clubs whose aim is to promote Zebra Finches or Bengalese on a more regional basis, and they also adopt the rules and standards formulated by the parent bodies.

It is important that only healthy birds in the best of condition are exhibited. Birds with missing, dirty or ragged plumage will stand little chance of gaining success and only reflect badly on their owner. With Zebra Finches it may well be necessary to cage them individually in the birdroom for about six weeks prior to the show season, and also throughout the show season, as cage mates will often indulge in feather plucking and general bickering. There is no harm in caging birds individually providing they are able to see or hear other birds of the same species.

Show cages must also be clean and well maintained. Usually it is necessary to allow birds to become accustomed to their show cages before being exhibited in competition. This is best done by placing a training cage, of similar dimensions to a show cage, in front of the stock cage door, so that birds can have free access to and from the show cage as they desire.

In order to promote better feather condition, exhibitors will sometimes spray their birds regularly with tepid water which has previously been boiled and allowed to cool. This spraying will be required about twice a week, although it should not be done within three days of the birds being exhibited. Often it is more convenient to keep a separate cage solely for the purpose of spraying birds as this practise can lead to stock cages becoming excessively damp.

At most shows there are champion and novice sections in which Zebra Finches or Bengalese can be entered. The terms champion and novice refer to the status of the exhibitors, rather than to the birds entered in the class. All beginners are regarded as novices and birds should not be entered in the champion classes. The reason for providing two separate sections is to allow new owners to compete without having to show their birds directly against those from very experienced breeders who have well established studs of show birds. Exhibitors are permitted to show their birds in the novice section for minimum period, usually five years, and will not be promoted to champion status unless they have won a predetermined number of awards.

It is usually necessary to purchase birds from an established breeder of exhibition stock in order to become a successful exhibitor. Birds bred in mixed collections seldom display the qualities desired in show birds. When first starting to establish your own stud it is advisable to concentrate on just one or two different colours, rather than trying to cover the whole spectrum of the mutations available. Exhibition quality birds cost no more to feed and care for, than do non-exhibition birds, and by breeding better quality stock it is much easier to sell surplus birds. Generally speaking exhibition birds may be a little more temperamental and it may be wise to gain a year or two years experience of keeping Zebra Finches or Bengalese before acquiring top quality stock.

Naturally there is a great deal to learn about exhibiting, much more than can be included here, but it can become a compulsive pastime and an eager newcomer will quickly learn the ropes.

10 Useful Addresses

The Zebra Finch Society
Mr. J. A. W. Prior (Secretary)
87, Winn Road
Lee
London SE12 9EY

The National Bengalese Fanciers Association
Mr. E. J. Hounslow (Secretary)
2, Bridge Street
Griffithstown
Gwent
Wales

Cage and Aviary Birds Magazine
Surrey House
1, Throwley Way
Sutton
Surrey SM1 4QQ

The National Council for Aviculture
Mr. J. A. W. Prior (Secretary)
87, Winn Road
Lee
London SE12 9EY

The N.C.A. is an organisation designed to protect the interests of all birdkeepers within the United Kingdom and to represent their viewpoint on a national basis.